Ninja CREAMi Cookbook for Beginners

Jane Averbah

CONTENTS

Introduction

The world has changed dramatically since the manual method of creating delicious treats was replaced by an electrical method. Ninja CREAMi, which has completely transformed the world of homemade treats, has recently been added to the list of electrical devices that can be used to create this unique and delicious treat.

This device, aptly dubbed a "frozen drink machine," is manufactured by Ninja CREAMi. It is a one-of-a-kind and groundbreaking product that has become the talk of the town. There are very few products available on the market today that are as distinctive as this one. With this revolutionary new product that eliminates the mess, you can easily cream your frozen treat, whether plain, flavoured, or sugared.

The machine is reasonably priced, and its straightforward design makes it simple to operate. You can come up with your own recipes or simply design a simple design for the favor you want to give. Designed for ease of use, the Ninja CREAMi features a clear, informative LCD screen that walks you through the entire process. This is made possible by the highly effective freezing mechanism in the Ninja CREAMi, which ensures that all of your ingredients are perfectly blended and transformed into a delectable frozen drink in minutes.

With a capacity of 4.5L, the Ninja CREAMi is simple to clean and can churn out a large number of drinks in a single sitting. In addition, the product's motor protection feature is unique. It ensures that the motor will not be damaged by continuous use while also ensuring the durability and longevity of your frozen drink machine.

This is a multipurpose product that can be used in any kitchen setting, including commercial kitchens. It creates the perfect frozen drink for any occasion, allowing you to enjoy your favorite beverages whenever you want them. Its cost is substantial enough to fit into most people's budgets. Therefore, it can appeal to any customer seeking convenience, affordability, and elegance all rolled into one package. It has been meticulously designed to meet the needs of the modern home, so you can rest assured that you are getting good value for your money when you purchase this ground-breaking product.

You can be confident that your frozen drink machine will be with you for many years to come because the Ninja CREAM is built to last and is built to last. Because of its small size and lightweight, it is easy to transport and does not take up much space. In addition, the machine is simple to keep up to date. It is used by people of all ages, from young to older adults, including the elderly, who may have difficulty lifting heavy objects due to physical limitations. As a result, it will be a suitable product for all types of consumers.

It is designed for people who are looking for quick results as well as convenience. There are no difficult manuals to read, and there are no difficult buttons to press in this game. Simply scoop the cream into the machine's specially designed cup, press the machine's button, and sit back and watch it work its magic.

Chapter 1: The Basics Of Ninja CREAMi

Healthy and creamy ice creams prepared in the comfort of one's own home are everyone's dream. But we understand how difficult it can be to deal with the entire process—having an ice cream maker certainly helps! The Ninja CREAMi Ice Cream Maker is one such appliance that can be used to churn all kinds of ice cream, sorbet, and smoothie ingredients together in a single container. So, to assist you in creating all manner of delectable freezer treats, we've compiled the best of the Ninja CREAMi recipe collection into this cookbook. Let's see what happens!

What Is The Ninja CREAMi?

Ninja CREAMi is an electric ice cream maker that makes delicious ice cream. Various frozen items such as smoothie bowls, milkshakes, sorbet, and ice cream are created using this freezing method. Although this is not a blender, it is a device that uses "creamify" technology to transform frozen foods into ice cream desserts.

When used in place of a blender, the Ninja CREAMi can do one of two things: it can either evenly blend all contents or do one of two things. Beginning with the Ninja CREAMi, combine all ingredients and process until smooth. Every component of the mixture will be evenly distributed if you use this method, which is comparable to a blender. For example, suppose you process chocolate chips. In that case, the chocolate chips will all be chopped up into extremely small pieces and evenly distributed throughout the mixture.

Pour the chocolate chips into the ice cream while still being mixed if you want them to be fully incorporated. During this step, the mix-ins are "folded" into the base. It is unlikely that you would get whole chocolate chips if you blended everything together.

The Features Of The Appliance

The power button is used to turn on and off the unit.

- Install Light: When the equipment is not properly assembled for use, the install light will illuminate. Make sure the bowl is correctly inserted if the light is blinking. Check that the paddle is installed if the light is solid.

- Progress Bar: It shows how far the One-Touch Program has progressed. All four progress bar LEDs will blink twice and then switch off when the program is finished.

- One-Touch Program is cleverly designed to prepare delicious items in 1-2V2 minutes. The length and speed of the program vary based on the best settings for getting flawlessly creamy results for that particular recipe.

- Ice cream: Assembled for dishes that are traditionally rich and decadent. Alternative recipes are great for making thick, creamy, scoop-able ice creams from dairy and dairy.

- Lite Ice Cream: this is designed for people who are health conscious and like to make ice cream with low fats and sugar. When processing keto or paleo, recipes can be chosen.

- Gelato: Mainly designed for Italian-style ice cream with a custard base. When specified, use GELATO to make delectable, delicious desserts.

- Sorbet: It is used to transform fruits that contain sugar and water into creamy delights.

- Smoothie Bowl: Designed for fruit (fresh or frozen) and/or vegetable (frozen) dishes that include dairy, dairy alternatives, or juice.

- Milkshake: Created to make thick, fast milkshakes. Simply pick MILKSHAKE and blend your favourite ice cream (store-bought or homemade), milk, and mix-ins.

- Mix-In: It is created to fold in pieces of candies, cookies, nuts, cereal, or frozen fruit to prepare a just-processed foundation or store-bought treat.

- Re-Spin: After executing one of the preset programs, this is designed to provide a smooth texture. When the base is very cold (below -7°F), and the texture is brittle rather than creamy, a RE-SPIN is frequently required

Steps To Using The Appliance

First, it is important to read the guidebook of the Ninja machine provided with it as it will guide about warnings before starting using it. Some tips for using Ninja Creami are:

- Using the ingredients, fill the CREAMi Pint halfway. Do not overfill the pint beyond the MAX FILL line on the label. Because this machine is not a blender, it cannot process solid blocks of ice or other similar materials. Smoothies cannot be made with frozen fruit or any other hard ingredients that have been processed; all fruits should be crushed before being blended together.

- If the ingredients for the recipe must be frozen, place the pint in the freezer for at least 24 hours after snapping the lid on. When it's freezing, some considerations to keep in mind are as follows: If your freezer's temperature can be adjusted, double-check that it has been done so correctly. Bases with a temperature range of 9°F to -7°F can be handled by the equipment on hand. Your pint should reach the proper temperature if your freezer is within this temperature range. It is necessary to freeze the base for at least 24 hours before being used in the processing. To avoid damaging your machine, do not freeze the pint at an angle while still frozen. Place the pint in the freezer on a level surface to expand.

- Place the device on a clean, dry, level surface, such as a countertop or table, and connect it to the power source using the included USB cable.

- Once the base is ready or frozen, remove the pint lid and place the pint in the outer bowl of the baking dish. Always smooth out the surface of a prepared dessert before refreezing it in a pint. If the pint has been frozen unevenly, place it in the refrigerator to allow the components to melt more evenly. Then whisk vigorously to ensure that all of the ingredients are thoroughly combined. Ensure the pint is placed on a level surface in the freezer before refreezing it.

- The CreamerizerTM Paddle is placed in the bottom of the outer bowl cover by pressing and holding the paddle clasp, which is located on the top of the lid, for several seconds. Release the lock to ensure that the paddle is secure. When the lock is fully attached, the paddle will be slightly loose, and the lock will be fixed.

- Place the lid's tab just to the right of the outer bowl handle so that the lines on the lid and handle are aligned with each other. Turn the lid counterclockwise to secure it.

- Check to see if the unit is connected to the power source. Finally, with the handle positioned below the control panel, attach the outer bowl to the motor base with the handle. To raise the platform and secure the bowl in place, turn the handle to the right until it locks into place. When the bowl has been fully inserted, you will hear a click in the machine.

- To turn on the unit, press the power button on the front of the unit. Suppose the outer bowl is correctly inserted into the machine. In that case, the One-Touch Programs will be displayed, and the machine will be ready to use. Select the program that is most appropriate for the recipe you are creating. When the function is completed, it will automatically turn off.

- Upon completion of the program, remove the outer bowl by twisting the handle back to the center while simultaneously pressing the bowl release button on the left side of the motor base (see illustration). As the handle is turned, the platform lowers the bowl into the bowl. Lifting the bowl will allow you to remove it.

- The lid unlocks button is pressed, and the lid is twisted in the opposite direction of the clock to remove it.

- Make a 1/2-inch wide hole in the bottom of the pint with a spoon if you include mix-ins in your recipe. To reprocess with the MIX-IN programs, fill the hole in the pint with chopped or broken mix-ins and repeat steps 6-10 until the mixture is smooth.

- If you do not wish to use mix-ins, RE-SPIN can be used to make a crumbly or powdered pint to make it creamier in texture. RE-SPIN is frequently required for extremely cold bases. Assuming the dessert is smooth and scoopable, carefully lift the pint out of the outer bowl and set it aside. It is necessary to repeat steps 6-10 with the RE-SPIN program to process the base again if it is crumbly or powdery.

Maintaining And Taking Care Of Your Appliance

Cleaning: To remove the CreamerizerTM Paddle from the outer bowl lid, clean the lid and then push the paddle latch before cleaning the lid again.

Before using them, containers, lids, and paddle should be washed by hand in warm, soapy water. To clean the paddle, take a dishwashing utensil with a handle and wash it with that. Thoroughly rinse and air-dry all of the components.

Prepare the dishwasher by separating the paddle, pint, outer bowl, and lids before putting them all in the dishwasher.

Remove the paddle from the outer bowl lid before cleaning it, as ingredients may become stuck to the paddle during the cleaning process. Then, thoroughly wash it with warm, soapy water using your hands.

Before you begin cleaning, unplug the motor base from the wall. Using a moist cloth, wipe down the motor's base. Avoid using abrasive rags, pads, and brushes if you want to clean the base. After each use, wipe the spindle beneath the control panel with a moist cloth to remove any dust or debris.

For cold storage, wrap the cable around the motor base and fasten it with the hook-and-loop fastener at the back of the motor base. When storing the cable, do not wrap it around the bottom of the base unit. Any remaining attachments should be stored next to the device or in a cabinet where the device's operation won't be damaged.

Resetting the Motor: This unit is equipped with a one-of-a-kind safety system that protects the motor and drives system from damage if they are accidentally overloaded. A brief period of inactivity will be experienced if the unit is overloaded. If this occurs, follow the steps outlined below to restore the device's factory settings:

- Disconnect the machine from the power source.
- Set aside for 15 minutes to allow the unit to cool.
- Take the outer bowl lid off and the paddle with it.
- Make sure the lid assembly isn't clogged with ingredients.

The Benefits of Your Ninja CREAMi

Let's look at some specific features and benefits of the Ninja CREAMi that show how special this appliance is.

Quick Processing Time

The machine chums the frozen ice cream mixture, breaking down ice crystals for the smoothest, creamiest ice cream, sorbet, and gelato.

Easy to Make Multiple Flavors

Make one basic vanilla base, then have fun creating two or three or six different flavors.

Make-Ahead Feature

You can make as many flavors of ice cream as you want ahead of time and just keep them in the freezer. Process the base in the CREAMi when you want to eat it.

Easy to Clean

All of the parts of the Ninja® CREAMi™ are dishwasher safe on the top rack, except for the part with the Dual Drive Motor. If you don't have a dishwasher, simply wash the parts with warm water and soap.

Smaller Batch Size

The smaller batch size means you don't have to store a big container of ice cream in your freezer. Just buy extra pint containers and have a tasting party or ice cream social with as many varieties as you like!

• Modes for Ice Cream, Sorbet, and Lite Ice Cream

You can make ice cream, gelato (Italian ice cream), sorbet (frozen and processed fruit or vegetable juice), and lite ice cream with just the touch of a button. Sorbets and smoothie bowls require more processing time at higher speeds to break up ice crystals for creamy results. You don't have to do any guesswork; no matter what you want to make, the machine does it all for you.

Chapter 2: Lite Ice Cream

Perfect Lite Apple Pie Ice Cream

Prep Time: 10 Minutes

Cooking Time: 24 Hours 5 Minutes

Number of Servings: 2

Ingredients:

- ½ teaspoon cinnamon

- 2 cups apples, chopped

- 1 teaspoon vanilla extract

- 5 tablespoons brown sugar

- 2 cups heavy crem

- ½ cup apple cider

Method:

1. Before putting a medium saucepan on the stove over medium heat, spray it with nonstick cooking spray. With 3 tablespoons of water, cook for about 10 minutes, or until the apples are soft and the water has evaporated.

2. In a saucepan, combine brown sugar, vanilla, and cinnamon. Cook for an additional 2-3 minutes, or until the apples are completely soft.

3. Transfer the cooked apple mixture to a large mixing bowl, then thoroughly combine the heavy cream and apple cider.

4. Fill a Creami Pint glass halfway with the base. Fill an ice bucket halfway with water. After it has cooled, cover the pint with the storage lid and freeze it for 24 hours.

5. Remove the pint from the freezer as well as the lid. Place a pint in the outer bowl, secure the lid component to the outer bowl, and place the Creamerizer Paddle on the lid of the outer bowl. To raise and lock the platform in place, place the bowl component on the motor base and twist the handle to the right.

6. For processing, select the Lite Ice Cream option.

7. Once the processing is complete, scoop it out of the pint and serve immediately.

Nutritional Values (Per Serving)

- Calories: 80

- Fat: 15 g

- Saturated Fat: 3 g

- Carbohydrates: 15 g

- Fiber: 2 g

- Sodium: 45 mg

- Protein: 2 g

Matcha Green Lite Ice Cream

Prep Time: 10 Minutes

Cooking Time: 24 Hours 5 Minutes

Number of Servings: 2

Ingredients:

- 1 teaspoon vanilla extract
- ½ teaspoon stevia
- 2 and ½ tablespoons raw agave
- 4 tablespoons matcha powder
- 1 cup whole milk
- 1 tablespoon cream cheese
- ¾ cup heavy cream

Method:

1. Microwave the cream cheese for 10 seconds in a large microwave-safe dish. Mix the stevia, matcha powder, agave, and vanilla extract in a mixing bowl using a spatula for 60 seconds or until the mixture resembles frosting.

2. Slowly fold in the heavy cream and milk until thoroughly combined and the sugar is dissolved.

3. Fill an empty creami Pint with a base. Place the storage lid on the pint and place it in the freezer for 24 hours.

4.   Take out the pint from the freezer and the lid from the pint. Put a pint in the outer dish, position the Creamerizer Paddle on the lid of the outer bowl, and secure the lid assembly to the outer dish.

5.   Put the dish assembly on the motor base and twist the handle to the right to raise and clamp the platform in position.

6.   Choose the Lite ice cream option.

7.   Once the processing is done, introduce the mix-ins or scoop out the ice cream from the pint and serve to enjoy.

1.

Nutritional Values (Per Serving)

- Calories: 170
- Fat: 17 g
- Saturated Fat: 3 g
- Carbohydrates: 17 g
- Fiber: 3 g
- Sodium: 122 mg
- Protein: 2 g

Lite Coconut Ice Cream

Prep Time: 10 Minutes

Cooking Time: 24 Hours 5 Minutes

Number of Servings: 2

Ingredients:

- ¼ cup stevia cane sugar
- 1 teaspoon vanilla extract
- 1 can coconut milk

Method:

1. Stir in and mix the coconut milk in a medium mixing bowl until smooth. Then, whisk in the remaining ingredients until well merged, and the stevia sugar is dissolved.

2. Fill an empty creami Pint with a base. Position a storage lid on a pint and put it in the freezer for 24 hours.

3. Remove the pint from the freezer and the lid from the pint. Put a pint in the outer dish and install the Creamerizer.

4. Position the paddle on the outer dish lid and secure the lid component to the outer dish.

5. Put the dish component on the motor platform and turn the handle to the right to raise and clamp the platform in position.

6. Choose the lite ice cream option.

7. Once the processing is done, introduce the mix-ins or scoop the ice cream from the pint and serve to enjoy.

<u>Nutritional Values (Per Serving)</u>

- Calories: 170

- Fat: 8 g

- Saturated Fat: 1 g

- Carbohydrates: 21 g

- Fiber: 3 g

- Sodium: 120 mg

- Protein: 2 g

Cinnamon Bun Lite Ice Cream

Prep Time: 10 Minutes

Cooking Time: 24 Hours 5 Minutes

Number of Servings: 2

Ingredients:

- ¾ cup heavy cream
- 2 and ½ tablespoons raw agave nectar
- 1 tablespoon cream cheese, soft
- 1 teaspoon ground cinnamon
- 1 teaspoon vanilla extract
- 1 cup whole milk

Method:

1. In a large microwave-safe bowl, microwave cream cheese for 10 seconds. With a spatula, stir together the agave nectar, vanilla extract, and ground cinnamon until the mixture resembles frosting, about 60 seconds.

2. Slowly whisk in the heavy cream and milk until the mixture is completely combined and the sugar has been dissolved.

3. Make a base in an empty creami Pint. Place a pint in the freezer for 24 hours with a storage lid on it.

4. Remove the pint from the freezer as well as the lid. Install the Creamerizer and a pint of milk in the outer dish.

5. Secure the lid component to the outer dish by placing the paddle on the outer bowl lid.

6. Place the dish component on the motor platform and raise and clamp the platform in place by turning the handle to the right.

7. Select the light ice cream option.

8. Remove the ice cream from the pint and serve immediately after processing.

Nutritional Values (Per Serving)

- Calories: 350

- Fat: 12 g

- Saturated Fat: 2 g

- Carbohydrates: 46 g

- Fiber: 2 g

- Sodium: 55 mg

- Protein: 5 g

Lite Peanut Butter Ice Cream

Prep Time: 10 Minutes

Cooking Time: 24 Hours 5 Minutes

Number of Servings: 2

Ingredients:

- 1/3 cup fat-free milk
- 1 teaspoon vanilla extract
- ¼ cup stevia-cane sugar blend
- 3 tablespoons peanut butter, smooth

Method:

1. In a medium mixing bowl, combine the milk, stevia blend, vanilla extract, and peanut butter until smooth, and the stevia is completely dissolved.
2. Allow the mixture to sit for about 5 minutes or until any foam has subsided. If the stevia isn't fully dissolved, stir it again.
3. Fill a clean creami Pint with the base. Position the storage lid on the container and place it in the chiller for 24 hours.
4. Take the pint out of the chiller and remove the lid. Place the pint in the Ninja creami's outer dish, insert the Creamerizer Paddle into the outer bowl lid, and secure the lid assembly to the outer dish.

5. Put the bowl assembly on the motor base and turn the handle to the right to raise and secure the platform. Choose the Lite Ice Cream option.

6. Take the ice cream out of the pint once the machine has finished processing. Serve right away.

Nutritional Values (Per Serving)

- Calories: 80

- Fat: 5 g

- Saturated Fat: 2 g

- Carbohydrates: 14 g

- Fiber: 2 g

- Sodium: 125 mg

- Protein: 5 g

Hearty Cookie Ice Cream

Prep Time: 10 Minutes

Cooking Time: 24 Hours 5 Minutes

Number of Servings: 2

Ingredients:

- 1 cup whole milk
- ¼ cup heavy cream
- 3 tablespoons raw agave nectar
- 1 teaspoon vanilla extract
- 2 tablespoons cocoa powder
- 1 teaspoon stevia
- 1 tablespoon cream cheese
- ¼ cup crushed sugar cookies

Method:

1. Place the cream cheese in a large microwave-safe bowl and heat high for 10 seconds.

2. Mix in the cocoa powder, stevia, agave, and vanilla. Microwave for 60 seconds more, or until the mixture resembles frosting.

3. Slowly whisk in the heavy cream and milk until the sugar has dissolved, and thoroughly mix the mixture.

4. Pour the base into a clean creami pint. Place the storage lid on the container and freeze for 24 hours.

5. Take the pint out of the freezer and remove the lid. Place the pint in the Ninja creami's outer bowl, insert the Creamerizer Paddle into the outer bowl lid, and secure the lid assembly to the outer bowl. Position the bowl component on the motor base, and turn the handle to the right to raise the platform and clamp it in position.

6. Choose the lite ice cream option.

7. Once the machine has finished processing, remove the lid. With a spoon, create a 1 V₂-inch-wide hole that reaches the bottom of the pint. During this process, it's okay if your treat goes above the max fill line. Add the crushed cookies to the hole in the pint. Replace the pint lid and select the mix-in function.

8. Once the machine has finished processing, remove the ice cream from the pint. Serve to enjoy

Nutritional Values (Per Serving)

- Calories: 150

- Fat: 4 g

- Saturated Fat: 1 g

- Carbohydrates: 25 g

- Fiber: 1 g

- Sodium: 65 mg

- Protein: 5 g

Blueberry Chia Seed Lite Ice Cream

Prep Time: 10 Minutes

Cooking Time: 24 Hours 5 Minutes

Number of Servings: 2

Ingredients:

- 2 tablespoons honey
- ¼ cup milk
- 1 cup blueberries
- ½ cup vanilla Greek yogurt
- 2 tablespoons Chia Seeds

Method:

1. Combine all ingredients in a large mixing bowl and stir until smooth.

2. Make a base in an empty creami Pint. Place a pint in the freezer for 24 hours with a storage lid on it.

3. Take the pint out of the freezer, as well as the lid. Fill the outer dish with a pint, place the Creamerizer Paddle on the outer bowl's lid, and secure the lid assembly to the outer dish. To raise and lock the platform in place, place the dish assembly on the motor platform and twist the handle to the right.

4. Select the light ice cream option. If some chia seeds stick to the pint's sides after processing, stir them out and re-spin.

5. After the ice cream has been processed, scoop it out of the pint and serve with your favorite toppings.

Nutritional Values (Per Serving)

- Calories: 123

- Fat: 7 g

- Saturated Fat: 1 g

- Carbohydrates: 13 g

- Fiber: 2 g

- Sodium: 80 mg

- Protein: 3 g

Chapter 3: Gelato

Cool Agave Gelato

Prep Time: 10 Minutes

Cooking Time: 24 Hours 5 Minutes

Number of Servings: 4

Ingredients:

- ½ cup unsweetened vegan creamer

- ¼ cup raw agave nectar

- ¾ cup soy milk, unsweetened

- ¼ cup caramels, chopped, for mix in

- 3 tablespoons granulated sugar

Method:

1. Begin preparing vegan eggs according to package directions.

2. Cook, occasionally stirring until the agave starts to caramelize, about 2 to 3 minutes in a pot over medium heat.

3. Remove the pan from the heat and gradually stir in the soy milk and vegan creamer.

4. Return the pan to a moderate flame and gently stir in the sugar and vegan eggs if used. Cook for 7 to 10 minutes, constantly stirring until the base temperature rises 175 °F on an instant-read thermometer.

5. Take off the heat and scoop into an empty creami Pint. Place a pint of water in an ice bucket. After cooling, place the storage lid on the pint and put it in the fridge for 24 hours.

6. Remove the pint from the freezer and remove the cap from the pint. Position a pint in the outer bowl, slide the Creamerizer Paddle onto the outer bowl lid, and secure the lid component to the outer bowl.

7. Put the bowl component on the motor base and turn the handle right to raise and clamp the platform in position.

8. Select the gelato option.

9. Make a 1 1/2-inch hole in the pint using a spoon. Fill the hole with chopped caramels and process the mix-ins program once more.

10.   Serve and enjoy.

Nutritional Values (Per Serving)

- Calories: 225
- Fat: 15 g
- Saturated Fat: 3 g
- Carbohydrates: 24 g
- Fiber: 2 g

- Sodium: 30 mg

- Protein: 8 g

Triple Choco-Creamy Gelato

Prep Time: 10 Minutes

Cooking Time: 24 Hours 5 Minutes

Number of Servings: 4

Ingredients:

- 1 tablespoon chocolate fudge topping
- 4 large egg yolks
- 2 tablespoons dark cocoa powder
- ¾ cup whole milk
- ¾ cup heavy cream
- 1/3 cup dark brown sugar
- 2 tablespoons chocolate chunks, chopped

Method:

1. Combine the egg yolks, sugar, cocoa powder, and chocolate fudge in a small saucepan and whisk until well combined and the sugar has disintegrated.
2. In a hot pan, combine the heavy cream and milk.
3. Place the pan over medium heat and stir with a spatula constantly. Cook until an instant-read thermometer registers 165oF - 175F.

4. Remove the base from the heat and gently stir in the chocolate chunks to melt and incorporate them into the base; once melted, strain into an empty creami Pint through a fine-mesh strainer.

5. Fill an ice bucket halfway with water. After it has cooled, cover the pint with the storage lid and chill it for 24 hours.

6. Remove the pint from the chiller, as well as the lid. Place a pint in the outer dish, secure the lid component to the outer bowl, and place the Creamerizer Paddle on the outer dish lid.

7. Place the bowl component on the motor platform and raise and clamp the platform in place by turning the handle to the right.

8. Select the gelato option.

9. When the processing is finished, add the mix-ins or, better yet, RESPIN if you prefer. The gelato should then be scooped out of the pint and served immediately.

Nutritional Values (Per Serving)

- Calories: 110
- Fat: 5 g
- Saturated Fat: 2 g
- Carbohydrates: 16 g
- Fiber: 2 g
- Sodium: 34 mg
- Protein: 2 g

Red Velvet Gelato

Prep Time: 10 Minutes

Cooking Time: 24 Hours 5 Minutes

Number of Servings: 4

Ingredients:

- 1/3 cup heavy cream
- 1 teaspoon red food coloring
- 2 tablespoons cocoa powder, unsweetened
- ¼ cup cream cheese
- ¼ cup granulated sugar
- 1 teaspoon vanilla extract
- 1 cup whole milk
- 4 large egg yolks

Method:

1. Fill a large dish halfway with ice water and place it apart.

2. Stir together the egg yolks, sugar, and cocoa powder in a small saucepan until all is merged and the sugar is dissolved. Do not do this in a hot environment.

3. Incorporate the milk, heavy cream, cream cheese, vanilla extract, and food colouring.

4. Heat the pan over medium-high heat. Cook, constantly whisking with a rubber spatula until an instant-read thermometer reads 165°F to 175°F.

5. Remove the pan from the heat and strain the base into a clean creami Pint using a fine-mesh strainer. Position the container carefully in the ready ice water bath, making sure not to spill any water into the base.

6. After the base has cooled, position the storage lid on the pint and put it in the freezer for 24 hours.

7. Take the pint out of the freezer and remove the lid. Put the pint in the Ninja creami's outer dish, insert the Creamerizer Paddle into the outer dish lid, and secure the lid component to the outer dish.

8. Position the bowl component on the motor platform and turn the handle to the right to raise and secure the platform. Choose the Gelato option.

9. Remove the gelato from the pint once the machine has concluded processing. Serve right away.

Nutritional Values (Per Serving)

- Calories: 240
- Fat: 5 g
- Saturated Fat: 2 g
- Carbohydrates: 45 g
- Fiber: 1 g
- Sodium: 55 mg
- Protein: 4 g

Pumpkin Pie Squash Gelato

Prep Time: 10 Minutes

Cooking Time: 24 Hours 5 Minutes

Number of Servings: 4

Ingredients:

- ½ teaspoon cinnamon
- 1 and ¾ cups milk
- ¼ tablespoon allspice
- Pinch of salt
- ¼ cup sugar, granulated
- ½ cup cooked butternut squash

Method:

1. Combine all ingredients in a small saucepan and cook over medium heat for 5 minutes or until the sugar has melted.
2. Make a base in an empty creami Pint. Place a pint in the refrigerator for 24 hours with a storage lid on it.
3. Take the frozen creami out of the freezer and place it on a plate. Install the Creamerizer and a pint of milk in the outer bowl. Secure the lid component to the outer bowl by placing the paddle on the outer bowl lid.

4. Place the bowl component on the motor base and raise and clamp the platform in place by turning the handle to the right.

5. Select the gelato option.

6. Once the processing is complete, take a scoop from the pint and serve.

Nutritional Values (Per Serving)

- Calories: 220

- Fat: 8 g

- Saturated Fat: 2 g

- Carbohydrates: 30 g

- Fiber: 3 g

- Sodium: 55 mg

- Protein: 3 g

Blueberry Cheesecake Gelato

Prep Time: 10 Minutes

Cooking Time: 24 Hours 5 Minutes

Number of Servings: 4

Ingredients:

- 3-6 drops of your desired food coloring
- 1 cup whole milk
- 3 tablespoons wild blueberry
- 3 cups heavy cream
- 4 large whole egg yolks
- ¼ cup cream cheese
- 3 tablespoons sugar

Method:

1. In a small pan, whisk together the egg yolks, sugar, vanilla extract, and blueberry preserves until thoroughly combined and the sugar is dissolved.
2. Mix together heavy cream, milk, and cream cheese in a hot pan.
3. Place a saucepan over medium heat and constantly stir with a whisk or a rubber spatula. Cook until the temperature on an instant-read thermometer reaches 165oF-175oF.

4. Take out the base from the heat and strain it into an unused creami Pint using a fine-mesh strainer. Alter the colour to your liking with food colouring. Pour a pint of water into an ice bath. After cooling, put the storage lid on the pint and place it in the freezer for 24 hours.

5. Remove the pint from the freezer and the lid from the pint. Please refer to the Quick Start Guide for bowl component and unit interaction information.

6. Choose the ice cream option.

7. Make a 3.75cm wide hole in the bottom of the pint using a spoon. Introduce 2 graham crackers, broken into 2.5cm pieces, into the hole and repeat the mix-in process. Serve right away.

Nutritional Values (Per Serving)

- Calories: 200
- Fat: 5 g
- Saturated Fat: 2 g
- Carbohydrates: 25 g
- Fiber: 3 g
- Sodium: 60 mg
- Protein: 3 g

Chapter 4: Sorbet

Banana Sorbet

Prep Time: 10 Minutes

Cooking Time: 24 Hours 5 Minutes

Number of Servings: 12

Ingredients:

- 2 teaspoons caramel sauce

- 1 frozen banana

- 1 teaspoon cold water

Method:

1. Add the banana, water, and caramel sauce into the ninja creami pint container and freeze in a cold freezer on a level surface for a total of 24 hours.

2. Remove the pint from the freezer after 24 hours. Take off the lid.

3. In the outer bowl, place the Ninja creami pint. Insert the outer bowl containing the pint into the Ninja creami machine and turn until the outer bowl locks into place.

4. Push the sorbet button. The sorbet function will mix together and become very creamy during the sorbet function. This should take approximately 2 minutes.

5. Once the sorbet function has ended, turn the outer bowl and release it from the ninja creami machine.

Nutritional Values (Per Serving)

- Calories: 70
- Fat: 0.2 g
- Saturated Fat: 0.1 g
- Carbohydrates: 18 g
- Fiber: 2 g
- Sodium: 25 mg
- Protein: 0.7 g

Hearty Blueberry Lemon Sorbet

Prep Time: 10 Minutes

Cooking Time: 24 Hours 5 Minutes

Number of Servings: 12

Ingredients:

- 1 and ½ cups lemonade

- 1 tablespoon cream cheese

- ¼ cup milk

- 1/3 cup blueberries

Method:

1. Whisk together the softened cream cheese and milk in a medium mixing bowl. Make a concerted effort to combine the two as much as possible. Some cream cheese bits may remain, but that's fine as long as they're small.

2. Stir in the lemonade thoroughly.

3. Fill the pint container halfway with the mixture, top with the blueberries, and freeze for 24 hours on a level surface in a cold freezer.

4. After 24 hours, take the pint out of the freezer. Remove the lid. Place the Ninja creami pint in the outer bowl.

5. In the Ninja creami machine, place the pint's outer bowl and turn until it locks into place. Choose sorbet as your dessert. The sorbet function will properly mix

and become very creamy during the sorbet function. This should take no more than two minutes.

6. Once the sorbet function is complete, turn the outer bowl and remove it from the Ninja creami machine.

7. It's time to eat your sorbet! Enjoy!

Nutritional Values (Per Serving)

- Calories: 256

- Fat: 7 g

- Saturated Fat: 2 g

- Carbohydrates: 56 g

- Fiber: 3 g

- Sodium: 96 mg

- Protein: 3 g

Pina Colada Sorbet

Prep Time: 10 Minutes

Cooking Time: 24 Hours 5 Minutes

Number of Servings: 12

Ingredients:

- ¾ cup pina colada mix

- 2 tablespoons sugar, granulated

- 1 and ½ cups frozen pineapple chunks

- ¼ cup rum

Method:

1. In a blender pitcher, combine all ingredients and pulse for 60 seconds, or until creamy.

2. Fill an empty creami Pint with a base. Place a storage lid on a pint and place it in the freezer for 24 hours.

3. Take the pint from the chiller and the lid from the pint. Place a pint in the outer bowl, position the Creamerizer Paddle on the lid of the outer bowl, and secure the lid assembly to the outer bowl.

4. Put the bowl assembly on the motor base and turn the handle to the right to raise and clamp the platform in position.

5. Choose the sorbet option.

6. Once the sorbet is done, scoop it from the freezer and serve immediately.

Nutritional Values (Per Serving)

- Calories: 288

- Fat: 10 g

- Saturated Fat: 4 g

- Carbohydrates: 50 g

- Fiber: 5 g

- Sodium: 9 mg

- Protein: 2 g

Cool Peach Sorbet

Prep Time: 10 Minutes

Cooking Time: 24 Hours 5 Minutes

Number of Servings: 12

Ingredients:

- 15 and ½ ounces peach, chunked

Method:

1. Pour the canned peaches (with their liquid) into a ninja creami pint container and freeze in a cold freezer on a level surface for a total of 24 hours.

2. Remove the pint from the freezer after 24 hours. Take off the lid. In the outer bowl, place the Ninja creami pint.

3. Insert the outer bowl containing the pint into the Ninja creami machine and turn until the outer bowl locks into place. Select the sorbet option. The sorbet will mix properly and become very creamy during the sorbet function. This should take about 2 minutes.

4. Turn the outer bowl and remove it from the ninja creami machine once the sorbet function has finished.

5. Your sorbet is ready to eat! Enjoy!

6. Serve immediately and introduce fresh mint.

Nutritional Values (Per Serving)

- Calories: 200

- Fat: 2 g

- Saturated Fat: 1 g

- Carbohydrates: 41 g

- Fiber: 3 g

- Sodium: 256 mg

- Protein: 4 g

Citrus Strawberry Beet Sorbet

Prep Time: 10 Minutes

Cooking Time: 24 Hours 5 Minutes

Number of Servings: 12

Ingredients:

- 1/3 cup orange juice
- 1/3 cup granulated sugar
- 1/3 cup beets, cooked, quartered
- 2 and 2/3 cups strawberries, quartered

Method:

1. Combine all ingredients in a blender pitcher and blend on high for 60 seconds or smooth.

2. Using a fine-mesh strainer, pour the base into an empty creami Pint. Place a pint in the refrigerator for 24 hours with a storage lid.

3. Remove the pint from the chiller, as well as the lid. Place a pint in the outer bowl, secure the lid component to the outer bowl, and place the Creamerizer Paddle on the lid of the outer bowl.

4. Place the bowl component on the motor base and raise and clamp the platform in place by turning the handle to the right.

5. Sorbet is the best option.

6. When the sorbet is ready, scoop it out of the pint and serve right away.

Nutritional Values (Per Serving)

- Calories: 24

- Fat: 0.1 g

- Saturated Fat: 0 g

- Carbohydrates: 6 g

- Fiber: 1 g

- Sodium: 2 mg

- Protein: 0.4 g

Clean Mango Sorbet

Prep Time: 10 Minutes

Cooking Time: 24 Hours 5 Minutes

Number of Servings: 12

Ingredients:

- 1 cup syrup
- 3 tablespoons fresh lime juice
- 4 cups mango, peeled, cubed

Method:

1. Put the fruit, syrup, and fresh lime juice into the ninja creami pint container and in a cold freezer on a level surface for a total of 24 hours.
2. Remove the pint from the freezer after 24 hours. Take off the lid.
3. In the outer bowl, place the Ninja creami pint. Insert the outer bowl containing the pint into the Ninja creami machine and turn until the outer bowl locks into position. Press the SORBET option. The sorbet will mix properly and until creamy during the sorbet function. This should take about 2 minutes.
4. Turn the outer bowl and remove it from the ninja creami machine once the sorbet function has finished.
5. Then, the sorbet is ready to eat! Enjoy!

Nutritional Values (Per Serving)

- Calories: 96

- Fat: 0.2 g

- Saturated Fat: 0.1 g

- Carbohydrates: 25 g

- Fiber: 2 g

- Sodium: 2 mg

- Protein: 0 g

Exotic Mojito Sorbet

Prep Time: 10 Minutes

Cooking Time: 24 Hours 5 Minutes

Number of Servings: 2

- 1 tablespoon rum

- ¾ cup citrus-flavored water

- ½ up water

- ½ cup white sugar

- ½ cup mint leaves, packed

- 1 teaspoon lime zest, grated

- ½ cup squeezed lime juice

Method:

1. In a mixing bowl, combine all ingredients and stir until the sugar is completely dissolved. Pour into a ninja CREAMi Pint container and freeze for a full 24 hours on a level surface in a cold freezer.

2. Remove the Pint from the freezer after 24 hours. Take off the lid.

3. In the outer bowl, place the Ninja CREAMi Pint. In the Ninja CREAMi machine, place the outer bowl with the Pint and turn until the outer bowl locks into place. Activate the SORBET function by pressing the SORBET button. The sorbet will mix together and become very creamy during the SORBET function. This should only take about 2 minutes.

4. Turn the outer bowl and remove it from the ninja CREAMi machine once the SORBET function has finished.

5. It's time to eat your sorbet! Enjoy!

Nutritional Values (Per Serving)

- Calories: 96

- Fat: 0.2 g

- Saturated Fat: 0.1 g

- Carbohydrates: 25 g

- Fiber: 2 g

- Sodium: 2 mg

- Protein: 0 g

Chapter 5: Ice Cream

Perfect Coconut Ice Cream

Prep Time: 10 Minutes

Cooking Time: 24 Hours 5 Minutes

Number of Servings: 2

Ingredients:

- 1 and ½ cups heavy cream

- 1 can cream of coconut

- 1 and ½ cups sweetened flaked coconut

- 1 cup milk

Method:

1. In a blender, introduce the milk and coconut cream and thoroughly mix.

2. Combine the heavy cream and flaked coconut in a mixing bowl, and then add to the milk-cream mixture. Combine well.

3. Freeze the mixture in an empty Ninja Creami pint container for 24 hours.

4. Remove the pint from the freezer after 24 hours. Take off the lid.

5. In the outer bowl, place the Ninja Creami pint. Insert the outer bowl containing the pint into the Ninja Creami machine and turn until the outer bowl is locked into place. Select the ice cream option.

6. Turn the outer bowl and remove it from the Ninja Creami machine once the ice cream function has finished.

7. Serve and enjoy.

Nutritional Values (Per Serving)

- Calories: 234

- Fat: 14 g

- Saturated Fat: 3 g

- Carbohydrates: 10 g

- Fiber: 2 g

- Sodium: 421 mg

- Protein: 4 g

Energetic Strawberry Ice Cream

Prep Time: 10 Minutes

Cooking Time: 24 Hours 5 Minutes

Number of Servings: 2

Ingredients:

- 6 strawberries, quarter cuts
- ¾ cup heavy whipping cream
- 1 tablespoon cream cheese
- 1 cup milk
- ½ cup sugar
- 1 teaspoon vanilla bean paste

Method:

1. Combine the cream cheese, sugar, and vanilla bean paste in a mixing dish. Using a whisk, blend all ingredients until they are thoroughly mixed and the sugar dissolves.

2. Introduce and mix the heavy whipping cream and milk in a mixing bowl. Whisk until all of the ingredients are thoroughly blended.

3. Pour the mixture into a pint container. Freeze for 24 hours after adding the strawberries to the pint, ensuring not go over the maximum fill line.

4. Take the pint out of the freezer after 24 hours. Take off the lid. Put the pint into the outer container.

5. Insert the outer bowl containing the pint into the Ninja Creami machine and turn until the outer bowl is locked into place. Select the ice cream option. The ice cream will mix and become very creamy during the ice cream function.

6. Turn the outer bowl and remove it from the Ninja Creami machine once the ice cream function has finished. Your ice cream is now ready for consumption! Enjoy!

7. Serve immediately, adding vanilla chips to support its flavour.

Nutritional Values (Per Serving)

- Calories: 105
- Fat: 79 g
- Saturated Fat: 10 g
- Carbohydrates: 79 g
- Fiber: 3 g
- Sodium: 221 mg
- Protein: 13 g

Caramel Creamy Awesome Coffee Ice Cream

Prep Time: 10 Minutes

Cooking Time: 24 Hours And 5 Minutes

Number of Servings: 12

Ingredients:

- ½ cup caramel syrup
- 2 cups heavy whipping cream
- ¼ cup coffee mate caramel macchiato creamer
- 2 teaspoons instant coffee granules

Method:

1. In a large mixing bowl of a stand mixer or a large mixing dish, combine all ingredients except the syrup.

2. Whip the heavy cream mixture until firm peaks form using an electric mixer. Make sure the whipped cream isn't "broken" or overmixed.

3. Freeze the mixture for 24 hours in an empty Ninja Creami pint container.

4. After 24 hours, take the pint out of the freezer. Remove the lid.

5. Place the Ninja Creami pint in the outer bowl. In the Ninja Creami machine, place the pint's outer bowl and turn until it is locked in place. Choose ice cream as your dessert.

6. Once the ice cream function has finished, turn the outer bowl and remove it from the Ninja Creami machine.

7. Serve with a nut of your choice as a garnish.

Nutritional Values (Per Serving)

- Calories: 186
- Fat: 16 g
- Saturated Fat: 4 g
- Carbohydrates: 3 g
- Fiber: 1 g
- Sodium: 56 mg
- Protein: 7 g

Blackberry Ice Cream Delight

Prep Time: 30 Minutes

Cooking Time: 24 Hours 5 Minutes

Number of Servings: 12

Ingredients:

- 1 teaspoon vanilla extract
- ½ teaspoon lemon zest
- ½ cup white sugar
- ½ cup whole milk
- 1-pint blackberries
- 2 cups heavy cream

Method:

1. Puree the blackberries, sugar, and lemon zest in a blender.
2. Put the puree in a mixing bowl after straining the seeds through a fine-mesh sieve.
3. Combine the cream, milk, and vanilla extract in a mixing bowl. Mix for about 30 seconds or until the mixture is whipped. Add to the puree and mix well.
4. Freeze the mixture in an empty Ninja Creami pint container for 24 hours.
5. Remove the pint from the freezer after 24 hours. Take off the lid.

6. In the outer bowl, place the Ninja Creami pint. Insert the outer bowl containing the pint into the Ninja Creami machine and turn until the outer bowl is locked into place. Activate the ICE CREAM button.

7. Turn the outer bowl and remove it from the Ninja Creami machine once the ice cream function has finished.

8. Serve and enjoy!

Nutritional Values (Per Serving)

- Calories: 560

- Fat: 7 g

- Saturated Fat: 2 g

- Carbohydrates: 3 g

- Fiber: 1 g

- Sodium: 58 mg

- Protein: 4 g

Delicious Chocolate Ice Cream

Prep Time: 10 Minutes

Cooking Time: 5 Minutes

Number of Servings: 12

Ingredients:

- ½ cup cocoa powder. Unsweetened
- 2 cups heavy cream
- 1 can condensed milk
- 1 teaspoon vanilla extract

Method:

1. Combine sweetened condensed milk, cocoa powder, and vanilla extract in a medium mixing container.
2. Whip the heavy cream in a separate container until firm peaks form (do not overbeat).
3. Freeze the mixture for 24 hours in an empty Ninja Creami pint container. After 24 hours, take the pint out of the freezer. Remove the lid.
4. Place the Ninja Creami pint in the outer bowl. In the Ninja Creami machine, place the pint's outer bowl and turn until it is locked in place.
5. Choose ice cream as your dessert. The ice cream will properly mix and become very creamy during the Ice Cream function.

6. Once the ice cream function has finished, turn the outer bowl and remove it from the Ninja Creami machine.

7. Serve immediately, with syrup or sprinkles as garnishes.

Nutritional Values (Per Serving)

- Calories: 100

- Fat: 15 g

- Saturated Fat: 3 g

- Carbohydrates: 18 g

- Fiber: 1 g

- Sodium: 156 mg

- Protein: 8 g

Vanilla Ice Cream

Prep Time: 10 Minutes

Cooking Time: 24 Hours 5 Minutes

Number of Servings: 12

Ingredients:

- 1 cup sugar
- ½ tablespoon cornflour
- 1 cup fresh cream
- 2 teaspoons vanilla essence
- 4 cups cold milk

Method:

1. Whisk together the corn flour and milk to make a smooth paste in a small container.

2. Introduce all of the ingredients in a mixing bowl and set aside. Mix in the remaining milk, vanilla extract, and sugar.

3. Freeze the mixture in an empty Ninja Creami pint container for 24 hours.

4. Remove the pint from the freezer after 24 hours. Take off the lid.

5. In the outer bowl, place the Ninja Creami pint. Insert the outer bowl containing the pint into the Ninja Creami machine and turn until the outer bowl is locked

into place. Select the ice cream option. During the ice cream function, the ice cream will mix properly and become very creamy.

6. Turn the outer bowl and remove it from the ninja creami machine once the ice cream function has finished.

7. Once done, serve immediately and add your preferred nuts.

Nutritional Values (Per Serving)

- Calories: 241

- Fat: 14 g

- Saturated Fat: 4 g

- Carbohydrates: 31 g

- Fiber: 4 g

- Sodium: 231 mg

- Protein: 9 g

Awesome Mango Ice Cream

Prep Time: 10 Minutes

Cooking Time: 24 Hours 5 Minutes

Number of Servings: 2

Ingredients:

- 1 cup milk

- ¾ cup heavy whip cream

- ¼ cup sugar

- 1 tablespoons cream cheese

- 1 mango

Method:

1. Combine the cream cheese and sugar in a mixing bowl. Whisk together all ingredients until they are thoroughly combined, and the sugar dissolves.

2. In a mixing bowl, combine the heavy whipping cream and milk. Whisk together all of the ingredients until they are completely combined.

3. Fill a ninja CREAMi Pint container halfway full with the mixture. Freeze 24 hours after adding the mango to the Pint to ensure you don't go over the maximum fill line.

4. Remove the pint from the freezer after 24 hours. Take off the cover.

5. Place the Ninja CREAMi Pint in the outer bowl. Place the outer bowl in the Ninja CREAMi machine with the Pint inside and turn until the outer bowl locks into place. You can activate the ICE CREAM feature by pressing the ICE CREAM button. During the ICE CREAM function, the ice cream will mix and become very creamy.

6. Once the ICE CREAM function has been completed, turn the outer bowl and remove it from the ninja CREAMi machine.

Nutritional Values (Per Serving)

- Calories: 229
- Fat: 10 g
- Saturated Fat: 2 g
- Carbohydrates: 23 g
- Fiber: 2 g
- Sodium: 312 mg
- Protein: 6 g

Cool Blackberry Ice Cream

Prep Time: 10 Minutes

Cooking Time: 24 Hours 5 Minutes

Number of Servings: 2

Ingredients:

- ½ pint fresh blackberries
- ¼ cup white sugar
- ½ teaspoon lemon zest
- 1 cup heavy cream
- ½ cup whole milk
- 1 teaspoon vanilla extract

Method:

1. Puree the blackberries, sugar, and lemon zest in a blender.

2. Put the puree in a mixing bowl after straining the seeds through a fine-mesh sieve.

3. Combine the cream, milk, and vanilla extract in a mixing bowl. Mix for about 30 seconds or until the mixture is whipped. Add to the puree and mix well.

4. Pour the mixture into an empty ninja CREAMi Pint container and freeze for 24 hours.

5. After 24 hours, remove the Pint from the freezer. Remove the lid.

6. Place the Ninja CREAMi Pint into the outer bowl. Next, place the outer bowl with the Pint into the ninja CREAMi machine and turn until the outer bowl locks into place. Then, push the ICE CREAM button.

7. Once the ICE CREAM function has ended, turn the outer bowl and release it from the ninja CREAMi machine.

Nutritional Values (Per Serving)

- Calories: 321

- Fat: 5 g

- Saturated Fat: 2 g

- Carbohydrates: 3 g

- Fiber: 1 g

- Sodium: 231 mg

- Protein: 8 g

Vanilla Chocolate Chip Ice Cream

Prep Time: 10 Minutes

Cooking Time: 24 Hours 5 Minutes

Number of Servings: 2

Ingredients:

- ¼ cup mini chocolate chips
- 1 cup whole milk
- ¼ cup heavy cream
- 1 teaspoon vanilla extract
- 1/3 cup granulated sugar
- 1 tablespoon cream cheese, soft

Method:

1. Microwave the cream cheese for 10 seconds in a large microwave-safe bowl. With a rubber spatula, blend in the sugar and vanilla extract until the mixture resembles frosting, about 60 seconds.

2. Gradually whisk in the heavy cream and milk until the mixture is smooth and the sugar is completely dissolved.

3. Fill a CREAMi Pint halfway with the base. Freeze for 24 hours with the Pint's storage lid on.

4. Remove the Pint from the freezer and remove the lid. Place the Pint in the outer bowl, secure the lid assembly, and attach the Creamerizer Paddle to the outer bowl's lid. The option to select is ICE CREAM.

5. With a spoon, make a 1 Vfe-inch wide hole in the bottom of the Pint. During this process, it's fine for your treat to press above the max fill line. Fill the hole in the Pint with chocolate chips and run the MIX- IN program once more.

6. Once the ice cream has finished processing, remove it from the Pint.

Nutritional Values (Per Serving)

- Calories: 450
- Fat: 5 g
- Saturated Fat: 1 g
- Carbohydrates: 22 g
- Fiber: 3 g
- Sodium: 341 mg
- Protein: 4 g

Chapter 6: Smoothie

Energetic Blueberry Smoothie

Prep Time: 10 Minutes

Cooking Time: 5 Minutes

Number of Servings: 2

Ingredients:

- 1 cup blueberry juice cocktail, chilled

- 1 cup vanilla frozen yogurt

- ¾ cup fresh blueberries

Method:

1. Puree the blueberries.

2. Put the pureed blueberries, blueberry juice cocktail, and yogurt into an empty ninja Creami pint Position the Ninja Creami pint into the outer container.

3. Put the outer container with the pint into the ninja Creami machine and turn until the outer bowl locks into place. Push the smoothie button. The ingredients will mix together during the smoothie function and become very creamy.

4. Once the smoothie process is done, turn the outer bowl and release it from the ninja Creami machine.

5. Scoop smoothie into a bowl. Serve immediately topped with fresh mint and fresh blueberries.

Nutritional Values (Per Serving)

- Calories: 206

- Fat: 1.5 g

- Saturated Fat: 0.2 g

- Carbohydrates: 42 g

- Fiber: 2 g

- Sodium: 103 mg

- Protein: 7 g

Peach And Cream Smoothie Delight

Prep Time: 10 Minutes

Cooking Time: 5 Minutes

Number of Servings: 2

Ingredients:

- 16 ounces can peaches, with juice

- ¼ cup vanilla yogurt

- 1 tablespoons agave nectar

Method:

1. Combine the peaches, juice, yogurt, and agave in a clean Creami Pint. Place the jar in the refrigerator for 24 hours with the storage lid on it.

2. Remove the pint from the chiller and the cap. Insert the Creamerizer Paddle into the outer bowl lid of the Ninja Creami, and secure the lid structure to the outer bowl.

3. Place the bowl structure on the motor platform and raise and secure it by turning the handle to the right. Select the Smoothie Bowl option from the drop-down menu.

4. Once the device has finished processing, disconnect the smoothie bowl from the pint. Serve immediately with desired garnishes.

Nutritional Values (Per Serving)

- Calories: 162

- Fat: 20 g

- Saturated Fat: 4 g

- Carbohydrates: 38 g

- Fiber: 53 g

- Sodium: 64 mg

- Protein: 5 g

Choco And Peanut Butter Banana Smoothie

Prep Time: 10 Minutes

Cooking Time: 5 Minutes

Number of Servings: 2

Ingredients:

- 2 large ripe bananas
- 2 tablespoons peanut butter
- 1/3 cup of milk
- Reddi-Wip Chocolate Dairy Whipped Topping
- 1 cup ice cubes
- ¾ ounces chocolate pudding

Method:

1. Puree the bananas in a large container and add all the other ingredients except whipped topping. Combine and put into the ninja Creami pint.

2. Place the pint into the outer container. Insert the outer bowl containing the pint into the Ninja Creami machine and turn until the outer bowl is locked into place. Select the smoothie option. The ingredients will combine to form a very creamy mixture.

3. Turn the outer bowl and remove it from the Ninja Creami machine once the smoothie function has finished.

4. Scoop the smoothie into glass bowls to serve.

Nutritional Values (Per Serving)

- Calories: 221

- Fat: 8 g

- Saturated Fat: 2 g

- Carbohydrates: 30 g

- Fiber: 2 g

- Sodium: 113 mg

- Protein: 4 g

The Great Gator Smoothie

Prep Time: 10 Minutes

Cooking Time: 5 Minutes

Number of Servings: 2

Ingredients:

- 2 Scoops Vanilla Ice Cream

- 2 cups ice cubes

- 2 cups grape-flavored sports drink

Method:

1. In an empty ninja Creami pint, combine the ice, sports drink, and ice cream.

2. In the outer container, place the Ninja Creami pint.

3. Place the pint in the outer container and turn the ninja Creami machine until the outer bowl locks into place. Select the smoothie option. The ingredients will blend together and become very creamy during the smoothie function.

4. Turn the outer bowl and remove it from the Ninja Creami machine once the smoothie function has finished.

5. Immediately pour into a glass cup and serve. Add as many nuts as you'd like on top.

Nutritional Values (Per Serving)

- Calories: 96

- Fat: 2 g

- Saturated Fat: 1 g

- Carbohydrates: 18 g

- Fiber: 1 g

- Sodium: 53 mg

- Protein: 1 g

Wholesome Avocado Smoothie

Prep Time: 10 Minutes

Cooking Time: 5 Minutes

Number of Servings: 2

Ingredients:

- 1 pitted avocado, ripe
- ½ cup vanilla yogurt
- 8 ice cubes
- 3 tablespoons honey
- 1 cup milk

Method:

1. Combine the avocado, milk, yogurt, honey, and ice cubes in an empty ninja Creami pint.

2. In the outer bowl, place the Ninja Creami pint. Insert the outer bowl containing the pint into the Ninja Creami machine and turn until the outer bowl is locked into place. Select the smoothie option.

3. The ingredients will combine and become very creamy during the smoothie function.

4. Turn the outer bowl and remove it from the Ninja Creami device once the smoothie function has concluded.

5. Pour the smoothie into glasses.

Nutritional Values (Per Serving)

- Calories: 96

- Fat: 2 g

- Saturated Fat: 1 g

- Carbohydrates: 6 g

- Fiber: 1 g

- Sodium: 156 mg

- Protein: 6 g

Chapter 7: Fascinating Milkshakes

Delicious Maple Pecan Milkshake

Prep Time: 10 Minutes

Cooking Time: 8-10 Minutes

Number of Servings: 2

Ingredients:

- ¼ cup pecans, chopped

- 2 tablespoons maple syrup

- 1 teaspoon ground cinnamon

- 1 and ½ cups vanilla ice cream

- Pinch of salt

- ½ cup soy milk

Method:

1. Fill an empty Creami Pint with ice cream.

2. Make a 12-inch-wide hole in the bottom of the pint with a spoon. Fill the hole with the remaining ingredients.

3. Position a pint in the outer dish, put the Creamerizer Paddle on the lid of the outer dish, and secure the lid structure to the outer dish. Put the bowl structure

on the motor base and turn the handle to the right to raise and clamp the platform in position.

4. Choose the milkshake option.

5. Once the processing is done, pour the milkshake from the pint and serve at once.

Nutritional Values (Per Serving)

- Calories: 90

- Fat: 1 g

- Saturated Fat: 0.2 g

- Carbohydrates: 13 g

- Fiber: 2 g

- Sodium: 100 mg

- Protein: 9 g

Cherry Chocolate Milkshake

Prep Time: 10 Minutes

Cooking Time: 5-10 Minutes

Number of Servings: 2

Ingredients:

- 1 and ½ cups chocolate ice cream
- ½ cup canned cherries
- ¼ cup whole milk

Method:

1. Fill an empty creami pint with all of the ingredients.
2. Place a pint in the outer bowl, place the Creamerizer Paddle on the lid of the outer bowl, and secure the lid component to the outer bowl. Place the bowl component on the motor base and raise and secure the platform with the lever.
3. Select the milkshake option from the drop-down menu.
4. Once the milkshake has finished processing, remove it from the pint.

Nutritional Values (Per Serving)

- Calories: 396
- Fat: 0.5 g
- Saturated Fat: 0.1 g
- Carbohydrates: 0.5 g

- Fiber: 0.1 g

- Sodium: 56 mg

- Protein: 9 g

Clean And Cool Vanilla Milkshake

Prep Time: 10 Minutes

Cooking Time: 5-10 Minutes

Number of Servings: 2

Ingredients:

- 4 large scoops of vanilla ice cream

- Whipped topping for garnish

- ¼ cup milk

Method:

1. Fill an empty creami pint with all of the ingredients.

2. Place the pint in the outer bowl, attach the Paddle to the lid of the outer bowl, and secure the lid component to the outer bowl. Place the bowl component on the motor base and raise and secure the platform with the lever.

3. If you want a milkshake, go for it.

4. Once the milkshake has finished processing, remove it from the pint.

5. Serve with a dollop of whipping cream on top.

Nutritional Values (Per Serving)

- Calories: 358

- Fat: 30 g

- Saturated Fat: 4 g

- Carbohydrates: 15 g

- Fiber: 3 g

- Sodium: 116 mg

- Protein: 8 g

Hearty Banana Milkshake

Prep Time: 10 Minutes

Cooking Time: 5-10 Minutes

Number of Servings: 2

Ingredients:

- 1 medium-size banana

- 2 tablespoons sugar

- 1 cup whole milk

Method:

1. Put all ingredients into an empty creami pint.

2. Position pint in outer bowl, install Creamerizer Paddle onto outer bowl lid, and lock the lid assembly on the outer bowl. Place the bowl component on the motor base and crank the lever to elevate and secure the platform in place.

3. Choose the milkshake option.

4. Remove the milkshake from the pint after the processing is finished.

5. Serve cold and enjoy.

Nutritional Values (Per Serving)

- Calories: 166

- Fat: 3 g

- Saturated Fat: 1 g

- Carbohydrates: 30 g

- Fiber: 3 g

- Sodium: 51 mg

- Protein: 6 g

Lemon Cookie Milkshake

Prep Time: 10 Minutes

Cooking Time: 5-10 Minutes

Number of Servings: 2

Ingredients:

- 3 lemon cream sandwich cookies
- 1 and ½ cups vanilla ice cream
- ¼ cup milk

Method:

1. In an empty creami pint, combine ice cream, lemon cream cookies, and milk.
2. Place the pint in the outer bowl, attach the Creamerizer Paddle to the outer container lid, and secure the outer bowl lid component. Place the bowl component on the motor base and raise and secure the platform with the lever.
3. If you want a milkshake, go for it.
4. After the milkshake has been processed, remove it from the pint.

Nutritional Values (Per Serving)

- Calories: 220
- Fat: 5 g
- Saturated Fat: 1 g
- Carbohydrates: 23 g

- Fiber: 2 g

- Sodium: 200 mg

- Protein: 1 g

Choco-Hazelnut Milkshake

Prep Time: 10 Minutes

Cooking Time: 8-10 Minutes

Number of Servings: 2

Ingredients:

- 1 and ½ cups chocolate ice cream
- ¼ cup hazelnut spread
- ½ cup whole milk

Method:

1. Place the ice cream in an empty creami pint.
2. Create a 1 Vi-inch broad hole in the bottom of the pint using a spoon. Fill the hole with the remaining ingredients.
3. Put a pint in the outer bowl, position the Creamerizer Paddle on the lid of the outer bowl, and secure the lid assembly to the outer bowl. Put the bowl assembly on the motor base and twist the handle to the right to raise and lock the platform in place.
4. Select the milkshake option.
5. Once the milkshake is done processing, take it from the pint and serve right away.

Nutritional Values (Per Serving)

- Calories: 516

- Fat: 22 g

- Saturated Fat: 5 g

- Carbohydrates: 70 g

- Fiber: 3 g

- Sodium: 200 mg

- Protein: 10 g

Coconut Chai Milkshake

Prep Time: 10 Minutes

Cooking Time: 8-10 Minutes

Number of Servings: 2

Ingredients:

- Ginger for garnish

- Ground cinnamon for garnish

- ½ cup coconut milk

- ½ cup vanilla coconut milk cream

- 2 chai tea bags

Method:

1. Introduce the coconut milk in a small pan over medium heat, simmer gently, and then take off the heat. Soak the chai tea bags inside the coconut milk until it reaches room temperature.

2. Press the tea bags into the coconut milk once it has cooled.

3. Fill an empty Creami Pint with ice cream.

4. Make a 12-inch-wide hole in the bottom of the pint with a spoon. Fill the hole with the chai coconut milk.

5. Place a pint in the outer bowl, place the Creamerizer Paddle on the outer bowl lid, and secure the lid structure to the outer bowl. Place the bowl structure

on the motor base and turn the handle to the right to raise and clamp the platform in position.

6.   Choose the milkshake option.

7.   Once the milkshake is done processing, take out the pint, then introduce ginger and cinnamon as garnish.

8.   Serve and enjoy.

Nutritional Values (Per Serving)

- Calories: 321

- Fat: 24 g

- Saturated Fat: 5 g

- Carbohydrates: 5 g

- Fiber: 2 g

- Sodium: 235 mg

- Protein: 9 g

Conclusion

The Ninja CREAMi is a professional-quality frozen treat maker that makes ice cream and frozen treats in minutes. To make delicious ice cream, sorbet, frozen yogurt, sherbet, or gelato at home, all you need is a refrigerator freezer and the Ninja CREAMi.

Give the Ninja CREAMI ice cream maker a try when it's time for dessert! You'll be glad you took the time to do so. It's ideal if you want a healthier alternative to store-bought treats, and it doesn't necessitate an expensive trip to the supermarket or health food store.

In just minutes, the Ninja CREAMI transforms your favorite healthy ingredients into a delicious frozen dessert. It's not just for making delicious treats; it's also quick, simple, and healthy, and it's a lot cheaper than buying the treat at the store. The machine has a separate canister that seals to keep the ice cream from melting while it is being stored.

Even when processing the frozen treat quickly, its broad stainless-steel base provides excellent stability. It also has an ultra-high-powered motor for quick churning and freezing, so you don't have to wait for parts to freeze before using them again.

This device can accommodate a wide range of ingredients and flavorings, giving you the freedom to make your own frozen treats. If you have a favorite frozen treat from another brand that you want to make at home, no problem. You can also experiment with different dairy, fruit, and other ingredients to create new flavors. Anyway, that's why this cookbook has you covered when it comes to reducing stress.

At the touch of a button, the Ninja CREAMi makes about 13 quarts of each product. To make professional-quality frozen treats, skip the time-consuming steps of weighing the ingredients, blending the mixture, and freezing it. This luxurious ice cream maker is ideal for busy households or kitchens without access to an automatic ice cream machine, thanks to its smooth exterior, simple controls, and small footprint.

Made in the USA
Las Vegas, NV
15 May 2022

48931399R00057